Follow the Circles
Instead of the Lines

Elizabeth Olson

ISBN:-10:1723113999
ISBN-13:9781723113994

DEDICATION

for Eric J. Seegel
1965 - 2017

Dear friend-
I still hear you

CONTENTS

ACKNOWLEDGEMENTS

A big shout out to my friends both old and new, my mentors, master teachers and family that pushed and prodded me along my path. I am forever grateful.

For the few who knew I was writing this book: thank you to Lael Jepson who treaded water while I stood on the high dive. To Diane Doering who helped me believe. My son, George Eric who is still teaching me in his own unique way that the universe laughs when we think we are in control. For my wolf pack of the long nine-week plan: Beth W, Julie, Jenn, Ashley, and Mary Lou —thank you for believing in our crew. For Mark, who never asked any questions. And a big hug to my Dad who saw pieces of me as a child that took me years to recognize.

For my long standing friends that influence me still by daring to live from their hearts: Julie Freedman and Scott Sandler, Will and Christina Skaskiw, Gail Sullivan and Jim Segal, Jill Gottfried and Alan Jacobs.

Much of this book was inspired by members of my sisterhood who each live their own courageous stories: BettyAnn Berejik, Mary Ann Somerville, Ali Sawyer, Linda Minisce, Avani-Jenn Vitalis, Fay DeAvignon, Herlda Senhouse, Kassi Sarante, Margaret Kelsey, Michele Milliken, Pam Giroux, Rita Nelson-Peters, Carol Meyer, Maggie Daigle, Isabel Umali, Cindy Moore, Lynne Parker, Nora Barnes, and Rita Nelson.

And last but not least, a special and heartfelt thank you to the maternal goddess influences in my life: my mom, Ginnie Panetta, Natalie Olson, Barbara Doering, Sharon Kaiser, and Ginny Seegel. In your own way you each helped me put some of my soul's pieces in the right place.

1 AWAKENING

Time to step up and step out
The universe rewards action, not thought
Stop thinking
Start playing-writing-creating-laughing-loving-living!
Embrace success AND failure
In fact, go fail
I dare you
Fail a lot!

Fail-rinse-repeat

That is the true secret to success

- How to Be Successful

You won't always be afraid.
It's not failure or judgement you fear
It's the abyss
that unknowingness
the blank canvas of the universe

The only way to know if it will catch you
is to take the leap of faith
stop thinking on it
count to three and fly

If your wings don't work
sing a song on the way down
look for a ripcord
say a prayer
but put it all out there

Otherwise

You die before you ever begin
surely that is the biggest sin
to die not ever having truly lived

-Feel the Fear and Do it Anyway

Not just another pretty face
a member of the human race
lucky to have been born
when it was surrounded by scorn.

Adopted. Given up. Surrendered.
Then chosen. Always remembered.
She knows no other way.
Her roots were transplanted.
She is loved many ways.

Always.

Like a firefly in the night sky
born to set free to fly.
Fly away to dream and grow
all the while forgetting to know
she was free to come and free to go;
Free to numb or free to glow.

The lucky one that got away
lived to shine and lived to play.
Free to learn, earn, give, and be.
In fertile soil she now blooms greatly.

- Adopted

Sing-song
afraid to do it wrong
Hell no, just let it flow
Choose or lose
Choose to step up
step out
embrace quiet
then shout!
Be heard

It's absurd, really, that I dim my light
so afraid to shine bright
I lived in a magic land in my head
because I didn't understand the world of people,
of churches with crosses and steeples

Knowing only that even as I struggle
we are all one
interconnected
regardless of gender, race, religion, social status
I long to belong
even as I construct that tricky, outer shell, layer after layer
and hold up my hand to keep out - stay away!

My heart craves to come home
Home to the ancient, rhythmic, drumming
The universal life force when my huge soul was safely
ensconced in a tiny place
miraculous in its very essence
just waiting for the right moment to scream into this world
and lay claim to a body and a mind and some free will, Baby
Sent here to remember
To remember to remember why I was sent here
Remember?

- Where is My Path Leading Me?

This is where the rubber hits the road
I waffle back and forth -
to and fro
A fork in the road
Hit the mother load
Or....Or...Or don't

Just stick with mediocrity
in good company
Who do I think I am to be special?
To be more than?

But why not?
Why not be the best of me?
It is not against-ness
It is not a competition to be better than others
but rather, a quality of being
of choosing
to be the best me I can be

That, my dear, can only enhance, not detract
When I shine, I attract
And yet, it seems a daily choice
I awake...do I choose to hit snooze?
Or seize the day?
Work or play?
Or put off the choices for another day...
and delay the process of becoming?

I am a result of all of my choices
And that, my friend, is why the choices scare me so...

- *On Choosing*

Now and again – but rarely-
I meet someone that sees right through me
That sees through my mask
into the heart of who I know I really am

And I am struck down
in a good way
In the way that says, "Stop playing your games.
Stop attempting to spin it.
I see what you're doing
and I want you to win it."

She laser focuses through the layers upon layers of fluff n stuff
and gets to that brilliant, shining, yearning, burning piece of life
that is aching to see the light of day

And I thank God we are on the phone
so she can't see the shocked look on my face
or the tears that spring so quickly and unexpectedly to my eyes
at the surprise of being found out
in such a gentle, forceful, yet spectacular way

It's like being introduced to my real self
again
for the very first time

-Grateful

I can't find my groove
the canvas is blank
I need a Think Tank
or maybe I just need to move.

I'm stuck; wading in cement
I hit a brick wall
and realize I'm not standing tall.

The doubt monster crept in
I was caught unaware
I looked in the mirror
I wasn't there!

Instead was a face
eyes lost in space.
I stared and stared
admitting I was scared.

I focused on her eyes
then to my surprise –
the shimmer of a tear
from admitting a fear.

And there she was
Back. Ready to play.
I didn't think I'd see you today.

"I'm always here," she said, "my dear,
But I'm only real when you feel
and that's when you heal.

Stop trying so hard and thinking so much
go run in the wind
feel its touch

See the ocean wave
watch the crows when they fly
you can live a whole life

In the blink of an eye."

She winked at me
and I stood up tall
vowing today I wouldn't play small.

With a bright smile
and a better vibe
I walked out the door
the chief of my tribe.

-How to Get Moving

Elizabeth Olson

If I can share a bit of my light with you
we make the whole world brighter.
Day by day
night by night
children in the dark become children with sight.

How awesome life would be
if the children could set the adults free
to believe in themselves like before they were three.

Before we learned words for this or that
Mom and Dad, dog and cat
When we still remembered the magic over there
but we got sent over here
introduced to fear.

Just to be clear…we all started in that place
then were given a body…a purpose…a face.

Then while we learn language
hear stories
both imagined and real
learn happiness and hurt
and are told how to feel
we start to forget what we came here to do.

-I Hope You Remember

Do a trust fall
Give it your all

Trust that you will fly
You've done it before
You howled at the moon and saw stars in the sky
You learned to walk, to crawl, to run
You rode the waves, laughed in the sun

You took the training wheels off
and flew down the street
up and down hills
life was so sweet
It can be just like that again
Embrace and allow a new story, a new thought, a new day
It begins that way

-Leap of Faith

Sick and tired of being sick and tired yet?
Perhaps it is time to get rewired and change my mindset.
Change my questions,
change my stories,
and I change my life.

Do I dare?

Maybe I don't care because my life is comfortable now.

What a trap
A load of crap.
Comfort is a sh*t show,
A whole lot of 'I don't knows'
of what I want or where to go.

But ah, if I did know, then what would it be?
Dig deep. It's there.

Fear masquerades as reality.

When the real reality is that I already know what to do and where to go.

-The Pain of Comfort

Relax!
I dare you.

Sit tight.

Just breathe.
(No really....b r e a t h e)

It's okay. Life was meant to be this way.

Chill.
No wine, no pills.
No fuss over spills.

Just down time – come around time.

Be gentle with yourself.
Tell yourself what you love.

Be grateful.
Be grateful.
Be grateful.

- Truth or Dare

She said with pride,
"I'm here.
I came to play this game of life.
This time I'm on the starting line,
never mind that it's past half time.
I'm here to play -- And not just play,"
She continued with a grin,
"Damn – I'm here to win!"

She can't play if she is just part of the crowd.
The onlookers – who just sit and judge
in their comfy, stadium chairs – they look but don't budge.

She is out there on the field,
under the lights;
She'll play for herself – and fight for her rights.
Then she shouts to the crowd,
"I'll play for you too!"
She laughs to herself – this feeling is new.
This confident, kick-ass attitude.
Not a minute too late.
Thank God she didn't wait again
and let the game go on without her.

Especially now that she's polished her skills.
She thinks about intuition and free will.
Her back straight, head held high, she stands tall on the field.
The rebel girl
runs out to play.

- *Take Back Your Life*

When you were born you were all knowing
coming from the light
script in hand for this time around.
The paradox is
That the more you grew, you forgot the things you knew
and you started to forget your lines.

- You Came Here for a Reason

She was living like a lion with a thorn in her paw
limping through life
waiting for someone else to fix it.
Until she realized
by removing the thorn herself
she could be unleashed.

-Wild Child

It takes courage to live
to keep going
face adversity
continue to give
to keep rising up when you fall

Imagine if you never fell at all

Where is the courage in that?
A life gone flat
No more feeling, reeling, dealing
and nothing appealing

-Lobotomy

What course will you chart
with your gift?
with your art?

Will you flirt with your muse
doing things that you choose?

Or keep doubting yourself,
put your gifts on a shelf,
for some time or later
or next time around,
after they bury you under the dark, cold ground?

Yes it's dramatic
but I want you to see
you can die while you're living
or you can live gracefully;
full of vigor and hope
giving back what you know.
You've learned it already:
you reap what you sow.

So sow, baby, sow
and do what you know!
Laugh like a fool
and live by new rules.
Bad habits were broken
you can feel the release.
That fact alone should bring you great peace.

Make your own deadlines
burn them down to the wire
but share with the world
your heart's true desire.

-Court Your Muse

Am I afraid to take up space? Use a pen that can't erase?
Let's get real, authentic, blessed with grace.
"YES!" I cried, "Let's find THAT place!"

Shed those expectations of perfection;
Be perfectly real.
Peel the onion.
Seal the deal.

Will I remember the learnings - heed the yearning?
Consider the charm used to disarm?

Judge if you must
you likely will - as we're wired that way.
Don't dismay
Someone loves you anyway.
Maybe it's you...
For me, that's true. Mostly.
And I continue to improve.

- Loving Myself

I am just now learning to listen.
But to really HEAR, I need to release and surrender.
I was holding on to my tightly held beliefs
that life was a serious business indeed.
How could I hear the songbirds sing, the peepers peep,
or the children at play while cleaning the toilets
and sweeping dust bunnies away?

I get dizzy when I forget to breathe – in and out – give and receive.
Balance – first take care of myself...so I can then take care of others.
I deserve to have fun and enjoy each day.
Jump in mud puddles; look at life in a sillier way.

When I not only flirt with happiness but court it in earnest,
it rushes into my life as if by magic.
I remember again that the pursuit of happiness is a myth.
It's not something out there to chase.
It's something I have within me
and then I bring it forth to share.
And so I am still learning.

-Learning to Listen

First she climbed the tree
that led to the roof of the barn
then she climbed onto the roof
avoiding the fire alarm

At the top of the roof was a set of stairs
spiraling up into the clouds
with an internal yes, she began her ascent
it was too late to turn back now

Up and around
Up and around
Through the mist
Not a soul to be found

All alone
yet she didn't falter
she knew a quest when she saw one
and when she viewed her fear as excitement
perhaps she could make this new quest fun

The wind grew stronger
rain pelted down
she picked up her pace
but she wouldn't back down

Up and around
Up and around
Through the mist
Not a soul to be found

The staircase shook
the steps grew slick
it swayed so much
she thought she'd be sick

She came to a door
she thought she knew from before
and she knocked and knocked

Elizabeth Olson

but no one replied
so she kicked down the door
and stepped inside

No one was home
she just saw more steps
and up to the attic
to the landing she leaped

The steps spiraled upward
through the ceiling and then
there she was in the clouds again

Up and around
Up and around
Through the mist
Not a soul to be found

She began to falter
She began to doubt
She started to cry and fuss and shout
but she remembered a quest could be this way
and resolved she wouldn't quit today

Up and around
Up and around
Through the mist
Not a soul to be found

Then she picked up a voice
on the wings of the wind
What brings you here on this night?
"I've spent half my life remembering", she blurted
"That I came here to share my light!"

She heard a chuckle in reply:
Child you're doing just fine
Always keep moving forward
And follow the circles instead of the lines

Up and around
Up and around
Through the mist
ALL the souls were found

They laughed and sang and clapped their hands
shouting "Better late than never!
Now turn around and go back down
And embrace your new endeavor
and this time if you please
you can do it with ease
and the grace of someone so clever."

She closed her eyes
and jumped on the slide
while they pulled the golden lever

And while she traveled back on a wing and a prayer
she embraced her Truth and accepted their dare
she no longer needed to fight.
She'd make it easy to share her light.

- *The Quest*

She awoke with a smile
first time in awhile
Child, you rock the world.

In her mental movie her old self became a blur
No longer a martyr
Her inner movie star began to stir
She could be a self-starter

Her own happily ever after
Shed happy tears
Embrace her fears
Then shower them with laughter

And shed them like the dragonfly sheds that creepy outer shell,
dries her wings,
and flies!

-On Changing

2 NOTICING

Elizabeth Olson

You will compare yourself to others and judge them and/or yourself.
The grass will seem greener.
It's all part of a lesson.

-Forgetting and Remembering

The Raven reminds me
that what I think I see is not always real.
Be careful, smart girl.

-Animal Messages

If the sum is greater than its parts…did the internet help – or hurt?

-A Web

Is she just saying that she likes my work
because she is an approval suck?
Stuck in needing to be liked, or hired, or whatever else she is selling?
Sniff what I'm smelling?

Or is that about me and insecurity?
Or not believing in ME enough?
Tough stuff.

Because it is just possible that just maybe
She is speaking her truth and dearly wants to assist in facilitating
that recently debilitating thing.

A midwife for my Becoming.
Birthing my brilliance.

-Questioning

All the signs will show up if you're ready to see them.

They are in the songs, in the woods, on the sidewalk, in the sky,
in the words of a passerby.

You really can't miss them

… if you're ready.

-Noticing

I'm afraid of the dark
because I come from the light.

So I will let there be light
and guard my spark closely.

-*My Treasure*

Elizabeth Olson

Are affirmations just a way to stir up conversations in my mind?
Conflicting inner dialects

Words intersecting with feeling of
"I'm just not there yet...?"

-Inner Critic

I can no long deny....I am free to fly and free to fall.
Free to fail and free to stall.
Free to choose to win or lose.

I can no longer deny...That I used to play small.
I used to slouch and watch mindless TV.
I let my job take chunks of me.
Of my time and of my soul
I'd give and they would take.
They'd pay
so I'd work
day after day
and forget to play,
denying that once restless, spunky inner child-
The one that ran free like a cat in the wild.

Now I stand in the dark on a midsummer night
and I stare at the stars in the sky
and I wonder –
where is she and who am I?

- It's Not Too Late

3 EMBRACING SISTERHOOD

Behind every man is a strong woman.

Behind each of those strong woman should be her man (or woman)
offering a soft place to land.

But that is not always the case.

-It Would be Nice

A hardass is a woman who hasn't integrated her feminine and masculine sides quite enough yet to become a Badass.

-Real Woman

There is the me that other people see
There is the me I see
And there is the me I am

-Multiple Selves

The cameras capture a beautiful princess with beautiful clothes
She lives in a bubble
and no one really knows what she is like behind the gown
when the cameras aren't around
Scheming how to slay her own dragon
Helping the ones who fell off the wagon
Plucking Humpty Dumpty from the wall before he falls
And reminding the prince she is a wise one, after all.

-Royalty of Women

Maine girls
Fearless
Running barefoot through the back yard
Chasing butterflies and picking up the creepy dragonfly discards
and the bugs out of spider webs
"Do you like books?" I ask.
"NO! We are ACTIVE.
WE'RE ATHLETIC!"

They don't need stories yet.

Don't fret.

They ARE the stories.

-Maine Girls

Decades ago, I learned my lessons well:
Another woman's man is wrong on all sides
in all ways and is everybody's living hell.
Lessons, lessons, we all fall down.
Judging doesn't change things.
Learn.
Let it go.
Forgive.
Go.

- Shaming

Blame game
Game of shame
Keeping secrets about relationships is lame
Name it and claim it
Or know to let it go.

-Learn

Elizabeth Olson

Don't dig through someone else's trash
Until you are sure it's been thrown out.
And then see if it is worth recycling before you take it home.

-Relationships

A true badass seeks to be her very best
And always
All-ways
Lifts a sister up.

-Sisterhood

ShadesofGray
Not as in the book or movie
As in the not quite #MeToo
Put yourself in their shoes.
See both sides.
I'm sure I'll get crap for this.

-Just a Thought

Sisters before misters
School degrees and things trump commitment rings
Chicks before dicks
Jobs before heartthrobs

-Rarely the Order of Things

Roomy
I barely remember college.
I didn't really fit in.
But oh, if I could do it over now.

We could be roommates again
and we would rule the school,
creating memories and living dreams
and using our knowledge for good.

-Mulligan

If only this
If only that
If onlys will always be
If only it hadn't been me.
 # MeToo

Elizabeth Olson

4 PARENTING

I wrote wisdom to a younger me
to free her from victim mentality
and from being so naïve for a smart girl
getting sucked into the drama world

Then I was a mother with ADD – not just my child but his father and me
A deficit disorder of attention re-ordered
accepting a truth of difference
and also magnificence

It's not an affliction for the faint of heart
yet it can be a challenge to finish what you start
in a brilliant, circular willful way

We weave through average
to seize the day

in our own time

in our own way.

-Game Changers

Parenting is just continuing to grow up
and learn life's lessons
the best you can
while simultaneously influencing your little audience
who never forgets -
and causes you to worry
and lose sleep
and question whether you're doing the right thing

I was told you are a good parent
if you question your parenting

If you didn't
you wouldn't care

And what does that say?

-They Don't Come with Instructions

I have everything I need.
What I do with these tools is up to me.
I wish I was better organized.

-Tool Box for Life

Being a good parent
means
doing the best you can
with the hand you've been dealt

Please do not judge one another

You may have no idea what cards someone really holds

- *Always a Gamble*

She made her choice
Or more likely it was made for her and she had no voice
as happens to women throughout the world
Left to wonder if her child was well
This is its own kind of hell

-A Child Surrendered

Elizabeth Olson

Your son is a BITER, they said.
(As a child, not now).
He will have to leave.

Another parent told me later that week
their son got kicked out too…
for throwing a chair out a plate glass window.

Those were the sweetest words I had ever heard.

-Daycare Trials

Middle school
A hell for kids and their parents
Kids are Bullies
Kids are Bullied
So many ways to play it.

Does resolution happen through actions or through words?

Are they acting out what they see on TV?
Bullies throughout history

What is the cause?
Humanity?

-How do we Help the Cowards Stop Bullying?

Why would this generation be like the last?
The only constant IS change.
Oh, and the tools are all different.
Oh, and the world isn't the same.

-Refrain

"If you do that again I will take it away."
"Go ahead," he said, "Take it. Take it all!"
As he slides his possessions across the table
And continues to march

To the beat

of

his

very

own

drum.

-Disciplining an ADD child

I told my son we should write a book together.
"I will write about what it is like to be a parent with ADHD
raising a kid with ADHD
and you can write it from your perspective."

"Right," he replies sarcastically, "because that would ever get finished..."

- Wise Child

Socially different
Frequently misunderstood
Square peg, round hole
Always my master teacher
When will I learn?

-ADHD

The mystery of ADHD
Did I find it or did it find me?

-Different

My son's soul came to teach
and never wanted to hear me preach
So I will listen
watch
pray
and maybe relax into understanding
someday

And sometimes I will still preach
and sometimes screech
and I will love all times
Everyday

-Patience and Love

I pray for my son
another best friend.
For this, will he shed his carefully crafted armor?
The chip on his shoulder
growing as he gets older?
If he dissolves the steel he feels protects his heart
giving me fits and starts
Does it answer his prayer or mine?
Do I believe it when he says he is fine?

-Always a Mother

Boredom is a sign that you need to ask yourself better questions.

-My Opinion

I believe in forward movement
yet I look back and see lack.
What would it be like to raise my son within the safety net of a loving
marriage?
What would it be like to **try** to get pregnant? To long for that?
Versus one year married, young, naïve, conceiving almost instantly
after barely giving the idea a nod.
Please don't tell anyone. It was so easy it's odd
when so many other parental candidates
are feverishly timing and charting
with a burning yearning for that union to take.
Who decides our fate?

What would it be like to lean into a relationship?
Me and him; us versus them?
A team.
That was my dream.

And yet, his father and I are still friends.
The co-parenting doesn't really end
even though our son is now a man.
It took years to understand that we are parents forever.

He chose us.
I guess that was always the plan.

We did the best we knew how.
In the rear view mirror it's easy to see different roads
yet all our decisions, choices, inner and outer voices led to now.
They were all precious years
and while the marriage didn't last
I am grateful the friendship did
and I can look back
and smile.

-Looking Back

Bounce back
Everything changes
The story rearranges
Embrace change
Gain a different perspective
Reflective
Nurture it
You are stronger than you know

-Wait For It

Autistic or artistic
Slim border
Fine line
Defective or divine
We label as crazy
the geniuses that change our world

-Embracing different

5 GRIEVING

Elizabeth Olson

I wish someone had something clever to say
to whisk away the awkwardness and pain

I slog through the haze of grief day after day
Some days are better than others

Other days start off okay and then some trigger blows me away

Mornings are the worst

I am as fragile as a soap bubble

-Grieving

Their voices whisper to me in the wind
Remember when...?"
Remember when...?"

My mom, gone 15 years
There is still pain in the laughter
sometimes tears
such is the legacy she left
Lessons I am still learning

Others joined her
relatives and friends
They glide to the other side
from various ends-
sickness, violence... it depends

And I am not sure they really end
because I hear them as they whisper in the wind

-I Can Hear You

Elizabeth Olson

I loved you on this side
I still feel you now
I seek your friendship still

I surrender to grief
Cracked wide open and shattered

And even as I mend
tending to the splintered pieces
and the reassembly of my broken self
I am only stronger sometimes

Yet I would never want it to be the same

And it never will be again

- Broken Pieces

I feel the portal opening
On the day nearing your death
But we didn't know exactly when you left
so perhaps it was one year ago today
and that is why you help the words flow out of me more freely

Pushing me in your gently way
like you used to do
when you believed in me so much more thoroughly than I could

And now I have to do that all by myself
except that you are with me still
and anyway -

You always believed I could do it on my own

- Anniversary

Elizabeth Olson

Let the tears come
flow freely

Breath

Feel deeply
the heartache that is grief.

-This sucks

You were my confidante
my fix-it friend
my mentor and wizard
of laughter and fears allayed
tending to nerves frayed

You lifted me up
and I was often amazed at your energy, your quick wit, and your spirit
Later, dismayed at your drug use, your habit,
your hidden dips into darkness you would never share
even when I said I would be there

It is so unfair
To you, to me, to family
You shared a bit of your shame
your blame
you were always so clever
but not quite so bright in the end

I forgive all that

I just miss you, my friend

-*Still Grieving*

You always knew the right thing to say.
I wish you could be here again – only healthy.
Is that selfish?

-The Universe Had Other Plans

You whisper in my ear
Like you are right by my side

If I could just reach through the veil
that separates here from there…

I'm stuck between hope and doubt

So I'll choose knowing.

- If I Could See You Again

Elizabeth Olson

Surrender
to grief
to life
to the present

Give it up and let it go

Only then will you know if you are free

-The Sweetness of Letting Go

The huge snapping turtle crawls up to the warm rock
in the middle of the lake
soaking up the rays

I saw him today

He's been doing that for years and he is still okay
Sometimes scared of others and sometimes others are scared of him

Today, he is tasting a spot of safety and comfort and warmth
on a God given day

And so am I

-One with Nature

Elizabeth Olson

Cardinals and owls and lions, oh my
A great blue heron flying by

Loved ones lost
saying Hi

Touching my heart as they grace the sky

-Signs From My Friends

Stuck between hope and doubt
A lot to think about
I pray for you to choose
Hope

-Choices

Elizabeth Olson

Learn from nature
Keep moving
Keep getting up
The spider will make her web over and over and over and over again

-Don't Quit

5 BECOMING WISER

Elizabeth Olson

I played a flirting game to lure them in
moths to a flame
longing to share my light

Almost instinctively
a quick wit lashed out
like a matador taunting a beast to the point of rage
while onlookers cheered, entertained

Did they know my wit was my shield I would wield when they got too
close to my heart?

I beckoned them to the castle
but the drawbridge was blocked

I thought I was safer in the palace alone

They could not get in

We all lost

-Steel heart

Carefully unwrap your heart
The self-made chains go round and round
Built up over the centuries
Lay down your sword

Choose the weapon of vulnerability
And the chains fall away like magic

-Freedom

She danced in the rain
and stomped in
every
single
puddle

She went on trail hikes
road her bike
did cartwheels and handstands
and squealed with delight

Slowing through the years
use it or lose it

She sits more
walks less
and runs barely at all

When she stands there is pain
and though the years have been kind
now she dances
in the rain
in her mind…

-The Good Old Days

What is she facing?
Facing the nation? No
Facing a sensation? Yes
She is facing herself
Facing the facts
Facing that she needs to act.

She looks in the mirror.
She does not see perfection…
She does not expect it there.
So she does not expect it elsewhere.

Long ago she surrendered to the realization-
The appreciation-
That to attempt perfection was a losing proposition.
She'd rather trust her intuition.
For what is a perfect daughter, sister, student, worker,
    wife, mother, or friend?
And why put that on oneself? To what end?

It is an unrealistic cloak of doom.
A set up – from which she got fed up.
Which is not to say that determination isn't warranted.
Striving for what we want is what we're all about.

She loves the quote stating our life is a gift from God
    and what we do with it is our gift back.
Kind of a sneak attack on free will and all that.

But the expectation of perfection? On that, she stood down.
Stood her ground.
Thank you but she'll pass.
Why choose that word when others hold a truer power?
Why not strive for capable, proficient, talented, or gifted?
When she sifted through other possible word picks.
Gifted is the one that sticks.
Gifted is the word she wanted to settle in her bones.

Looking closely
She sees a wise reality.
Smile lines that define the woman she has come to be.

Wisdom lines, if you will.
And age spots. She studies the age spots.
Memory dots, she calls them.

Of simple fun in the sun

Moments on her timeline, etched into fine lines
So that she can remember that life is a continual process
Of earning and yearning and learning.

Of becoming capable, talented, or just testing the waters
Telling stories to our sons and daughters.

Teaching them to know it is fun to show up to the show.
To walk on the stage and make a debut
Have fun; take their cue.

And be okay falling flat on their faces.
Being perfectly imperfect is not a disgrace.
Rather, to dare greatly and often fail creates the path that enables the
tales we share with our sons and daughters of the future.

The bumps, the bruises,
the scars, the sutures
that create the lines, and the spots of introspection
that she faces now in her reflection.

-What are you looking at?

You know you are squarely in the midst of middle-age
when your bathing suit bottom has a skirt attached.
But hey-
above ground is a good day.

- Dress for the Body you Have not the Body you Want

Gravity wins.

-*Constant*

Nay Nay
Turns to Yay-Yay
Awareness
What's your story?
Do you awake with a smile on your face
full of sass and glory?

Yay yay
Do it your way.
What a load of crap some days.

-Fine Line

I believed in magic for a long time
before anyone told me there was no such thing

-They Were Wrong

When my dad was my age now
I thought he was old
As I watch life unfold
I see I was wrong

-Wiser With Age

In search of the right man she was reminded…
'Dear, Jesus is dead'
But hadn't she herself walked on water once?

Granted, it was ice at the time.

And thin.

On a below freezing day.

Not too wise.

So what was she really wanting?

- Looking for Mr. Right

Is your heart on fire?

You mean like heartburn?

No, I mean like passion.

Your choice.

-Passion or Antacids

Today I discovered how to get in touch with an old friend.
We haven't spoken in a long, long time.
She went her way and I went mine.

I don't recall a rift
We just seemed to drift apart.
I guess it was the busy-ness of life.

I wonder how she is now
Is she a mother? A wife?
Will she want to hear from me?
Has it been too long?
Did I do something wrong?

I pretend I don't care.
Then I muster my courage
and call.

Turns out she wasn't upset at all.
We talked for hours.
Bridging a decades long gap in a short time.

And now I have her number
and she has mine.

-Reconnect

Ladybug, Ladybug fly away home
Your house is just fine
and your children are waiting for you to teach them how to play

- Reframe

Elizabeth Olson

From landlines to iPhones
used to be just no one home

Today we have an instant reach
hard to avoid
easier to teach
From buildings to online schools
Change lives by changing tools

Who are the chiefs and who are the fools?
From books to e-readers
Some say we have wimps as leaders

Does anyone know where the good ones go?

-*Game Changers Again*

One boat
one couple
plus two dogs
equals
more than twelve relationships

-New Math

Re-write your script
Practice your lines

Not the ones on our face
The ones in your mind

Redefine you – stand tall
Thicken your skin
Don't look out there
Look within

Deflect negativity
If it's seen in you – it is only because they have it too

-Be Strong

Be your own best friend
like you are the last person on earth
about to meet the other last person in the world
that you didn't know was there
Be your best self
that you would never want to discount or discard

-Self-Love

Elizabeth Olson

What is your body's natural state from cartwheels to canes

Running on empty?

What fills your tank?

Fuels your body?

Feeds you mind?

-*Questions Change Your Life*

7 WORKING

The project manager asks if I have a good lessons learned document I can send her.

I forwarded my resume.

-LOL

Fake greetings and ineffective meetings

and some executives say
"We appreciate you and all you did today"

Of course they do
I would too
If you worked like a dog for me
I might even rid you of fleas

The undead dead
Monday mornings of dread
By Friday they're too tired to play
I understand why people walk away

Some over eager leaders
jockeying to please
as they chase golden handcuffs,
promotions and such
It's all a bit much.

The walking zombie apocalypse marches to work each day
Grabbing caffeine along the way and slogging through,
they work to pay for accumulated debt
from unwise choices or nagging voices
thinking bigger was better and more is good
They shouldn't have bought it but they knew they would
Consumerism, spending, greed
Dudes…please - change your creed

She played their game but she played hers too
She did her job well; She saw it through
She was wowed and rewarded
Kowtowed and cavorted

And all the while she worked with a smile
because her work was a game
almost a dare
She worked enough to be more than fair
yet not too much to really care.

She woke up her teammates
coaxed them out of their shells
Sometimes she'd swear just to see if they'd tell

Then one day with a spring in her step
and a smile on her face
she left that place without a trace

And the zombies went back to their sneak attack
to jobs that left them with a sense of lack

She now sharpens her carefully crafted tools
updating her spreadsheets and plans

She sends an invite for a different sort of meeting
And hopes people understand

-Job vs. Calling

Everyone else seems so confident with their carefully crafted resumes
Those three precious letters from universities
The bold job titles and bullets of success
that makes me want to shout in jest: "REALLY?
THIS is what makes you proud!?"

I want to laugh out loud
Don't you get it?
This one page list of life
no mention of kids, a husband or wife
or a kindness shown
a true change made
with a human touch
a life well played
Where you touched someone's heart
or climbed up from a hole
When you came face to face with the depth of your soul

PLEASE
Tell me
Why should I hire you to be in my life?

-Why Are You Really Here?

Do you link your possessions to your success?

-Values

Dial up the vulnerability
Try it on for size
Feel your comfort meter shrink
Get your hands dirty
That's playing both sides
Being all aggressive and masculine
Then stopping and slowly showing your soft underbelly
Don't move

Watch this impact the organization
silently following like newly tipped dominos
who can't help but be touched.

-Feminine Leadership

Elizabeth Olson

From Russia with lies
Stormy skies
Expensive phone booths
And investigations of fraud
I find it all very, very odd.

-*Politics and News*

Sometimes I'm better off not knowing
what is going on in the rest of the world
and just influencing mine with kindness.

True kindness is a super power.
It could change the rest of the world.

Sometimes I am not kind.

-I Do My Best

Write
with feverish delight!
Like your brain itches
and the only way to scratch is to scrawl
Let the words leak out
then jump and shout onto the page

Let them flow
get engaged
be bold
There are so many things that need to be told

They're lined up
some solo
some two by two
some are pushing and shoving to get through
others are shy but won't be denied
Free them all!

Let them overflow from the wellspring
fertilize the land
let the words take a stand
As we march
march
march
toward a different world.

- A Tidal Wave of Words

Bits and pieces of moments in time
How to choose what to share
She gives and gives
Telling more and more

Hard to choose what to leave on the cutting room floor

- *My Stories*

Elizabeth Olson

Calling all writers

Name it
Claim it
Don't fuss with a need for fame
Dare to share
To resonate
Raise the vibration of a damaged nation
one
word
at
a
time

-*The World Needs Your Gifts*

ABOUT THE AUTHOR

Elizabeth Olson lives outside of Portland, Maine where she can be found howling with her two sled dogs, staking out foxes and fireflies, pretending to be proper while combating mediocrity, and finally proclaiming herself one of the cool kids, despite being middle-aged and devoid of tattoos.

Often accused of being an optimist with a healthy dose of quick-witted sarcasm, Elizabeth embraces the challenges of life, liberty, and the pursuit of what makes people tick.

If you have questions or would like more information:
elizabetholsonauthor@gmail.com

Made in the USA
Middletown, DE
11 August 2018